HISTORY OF INVENTIONS

Road Transportation

From Carts to Racing Cars

Tracey Kelly

I0893905

BROWN BEAR BOOKS

Published by Brown Bear Books Ltd
4877 N. Circulo Bujia
Tucson, AZ 85718
USA

and

Unit 1/D, Leroy House
436 Essex Rd
London N1 3QP
UK

ISBN 978-1-78121-453-4 (library bound)
ISBN 978-1-78121-469-5 (paperback)

Library of Congress Cataloging-in-Publication Data available on request

Text: Tracey Kelly
Designer: Supriya Sahai
Design Manager: Keith Davis
Picture Manager: Sophie Mortimer
Editorial Director: Lindsey Lowe
Children's Publisher: Anne O'Daly

Picture Credits
Front Cover: Shutterstock: Tonicav.
Alamy: Granger Historical Picture Archive, 7, INTERFOTO, 9; Brown Bear Books: 5t, 17; iStock: 9, 20, 21, cipango27, 18, duncan1890, 6, Laocracio, 14, Phooey, 5b, Tonpicknick, 16; Mary Evans: 12; Public Domain: 8, DeFacto, 13, The Story of Ford, 9; Shutterstock: Ashwin, 4, Bright, 15, Ivan Garcia, 19, Rob Wilson, 11.
Key: t=top, b=bottom, c=center, l=left, r=right

Brown Bear Books has made every attempt to contact the copyright holder.
If you have any information, please contact: licensing@brownbearbooks.co.uk

Manufactured in the United States of America
CPSIA compliance information: Batch#AG/5624

Websites
The website addresses in this book were valid at the time of going to press. However, it is possible that contents or addresses may change following publication of this book. No responsibility for any such changes can be accepted by the author or the publisher. Readers should be supervised when they access the Internet.

Contents

Getting Around

Cars were invented more than 100 years ago. But people got around before that! The wheel was invented about 6,000 years ago. Then, people built carts to carry things and move around.

Egyptian Carts

Carts and chariots were used 3,500 years ago in ancient Egypt. This chariot had two wheels. Two horses pulled it. It was very fast!

Roman Roads

The ancient Romans lived 2,000 years ago. They built many roads. The roads were paved with stones. That kept heavy carts from sinking in the mud.

Stagecoaches

The stagecoach was used from the 1640s in England. Passengers sat inside a closed carriage. Four horses pulled the coach. A stagecoach could travel 60 miles (100 kilometers) a day.

Read on ... to learn about how people got around through the years.

Steam Wagon

Early vehicles were pulled by animals or people. Then, people invented the steam engine. The steam wagon had a steam engine. A driver pulled a lever to start and stop.

Mines and Factories
Steam engines powered vehicles. They also made machines work in mines and factories. This machine is working in a factory.

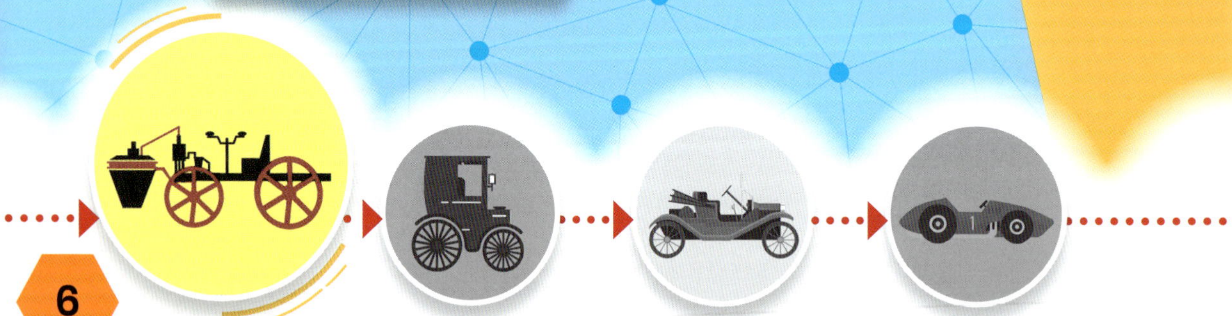

Steam Engine
Steam engines worked using steam power. Water was boiled, which made steam. The steam made the engine parts move. This pushed the wagon forward.

Horseless Carriage

The first cars were called "horseless carriages." They still looked like carriages. But they didn't need horses to pull them!

Pumped-Up Tires
Old tires were solid. They made the ride bumpy. People started using air-filled tires. They had a rubber tube inside, pumped up with air. This made driving smoother!

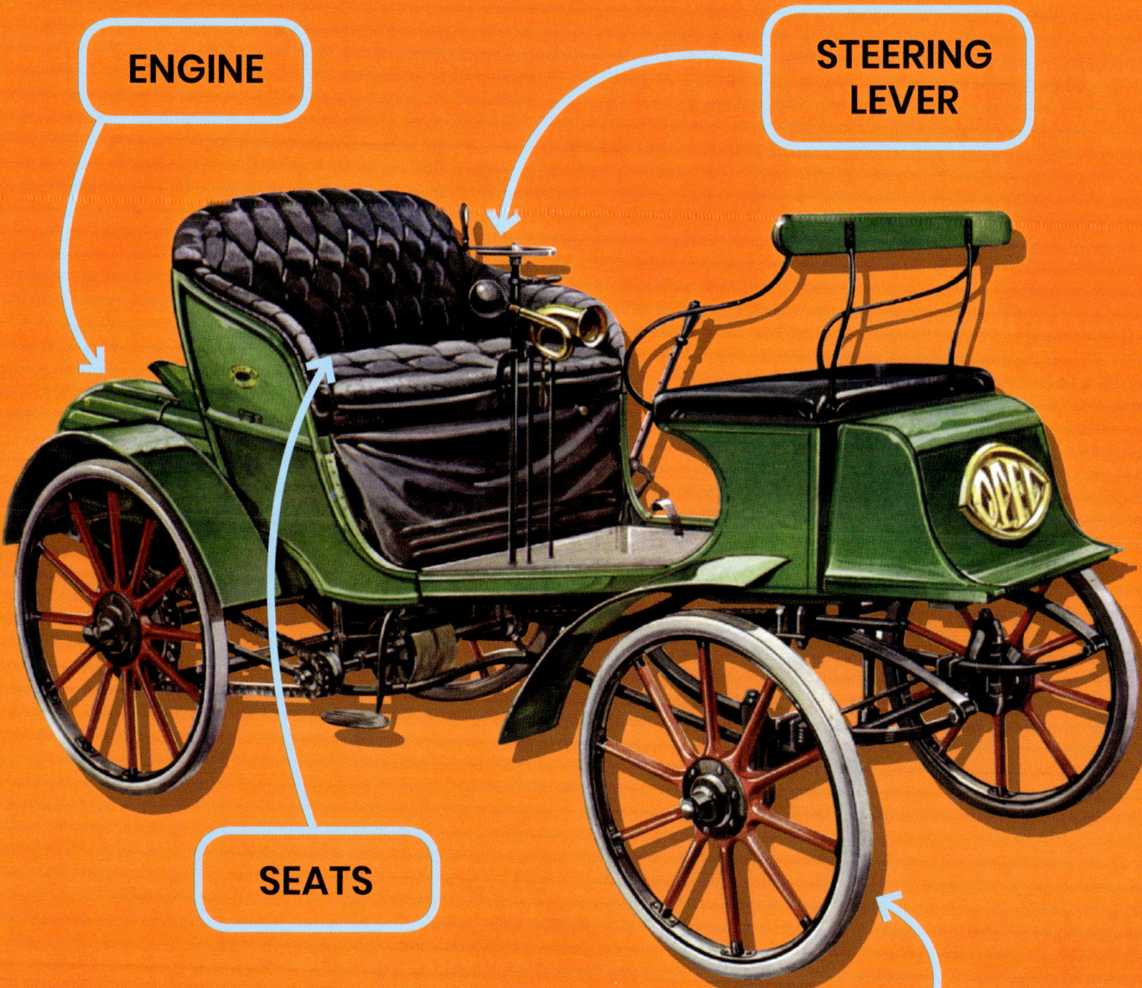

Combustion Engine
Cars had a new kind of engine. It was called a combustion engine. Combustion means “burning.” The engine burned fuel to make the car move.

Model T Ford

The Model T Ford was the first car that families could afford. It was very popular. The Model T ran on gasoline. It could go up to 45 miles (72 kilometers) per hour.

Assembly Line
Model T Fords were built on an assembly line. Workers added parts to each car. Then, other workers added more parts. Cars were built very fast.

Model T Factory

Henry Ford built a factory. It made 15 million Model T cars between 1908 and 1927! They all looked the same.

Sports Car

Car engines became more powerful in the 1920s. People liked driving fast for fun, or "sport." So, sports cars were invented. They looked very stylish, too.

Traffic Lights

More cars were on the road. So, traffic lights were invented to control traffic. They had red, yellow, and green lights. Timers switched between the colors.

Jaguar SS100

The Jaguar SS100 was an early sports car. It could drive 100 miles (160 kilometers) per hour! It had a top that went up or down. The engine was under the hood.

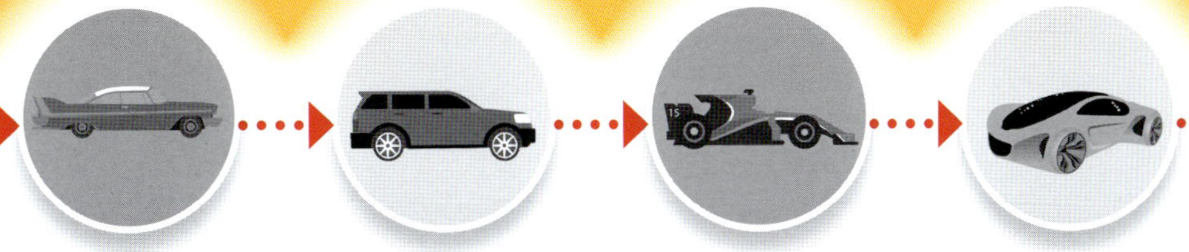

Big Car

Big cars were built for driving long distances. They were comfortable and easy to drive. There were seat belts for safety. Air conditioners kept the car cool in hot weather!

Road Trips
Highways are long-distance roads. The longest highway in the United States is 3,365 miles (5,415 kilometers) long! It stretches from Portland, Oregon, to Boston.

Cadillac

The Cadillac hardtop looked sleek. It had decorations called tail fins. You could listen to the radio. People wanted one in the 1960s.

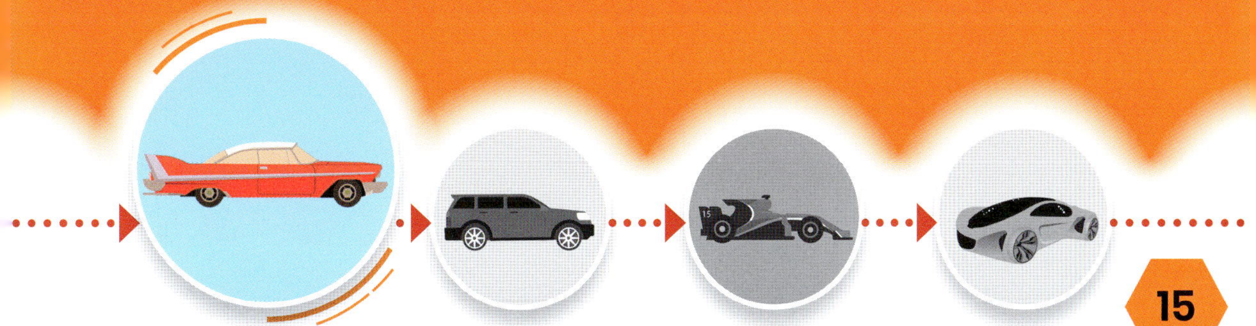

Computer Control

Today, cars use computers. The computer controls the engine. It helps with driving. Some cars have GPS on the dashboard.

Cleaner Fuels
Gasoline causes pollution. New fuels are being used. Some cars run on fuel made from plants! Electric cars run on electricity. You plug them in to charge the battery.

Safety First

Modern cars have thousands of parts! They have safety features, such as air bags. These inflate and protect people in a crash.

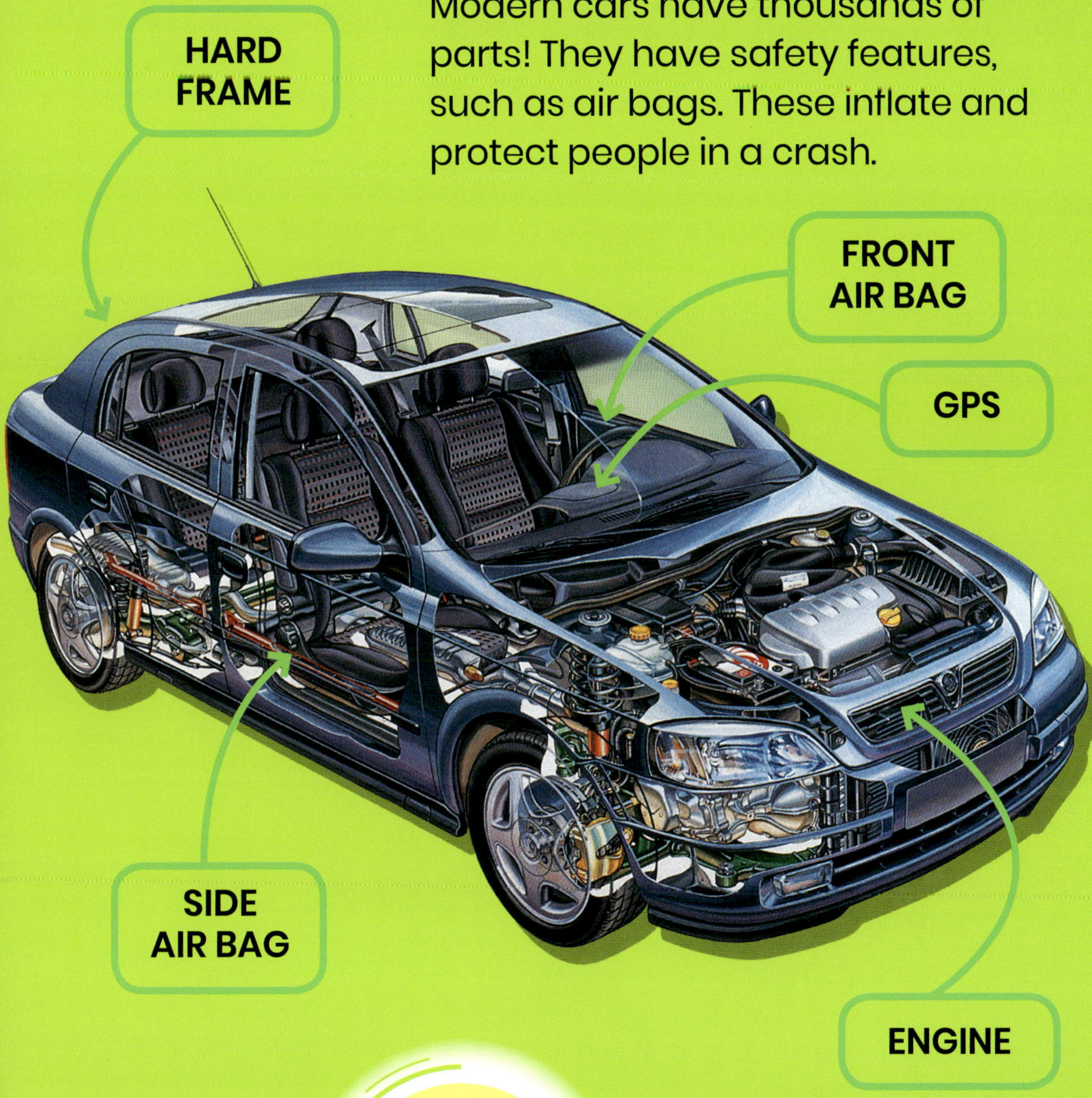

Race Car

Formula 1 race cars are built for speed. They can go up to 217 miles (350 kilometers) per hour. The body is close to the ground. It is shaped like a wedge. It can cut through the air that moves against it.

Tire Treads
Tires need to grip the road in the rain. So, they are made with deep tread patterns.

Formula 1 Race Car

A race car has a powerful engine. The driver sits in the cockpit. The frame has to be extra strong. This keeps the driver safe.

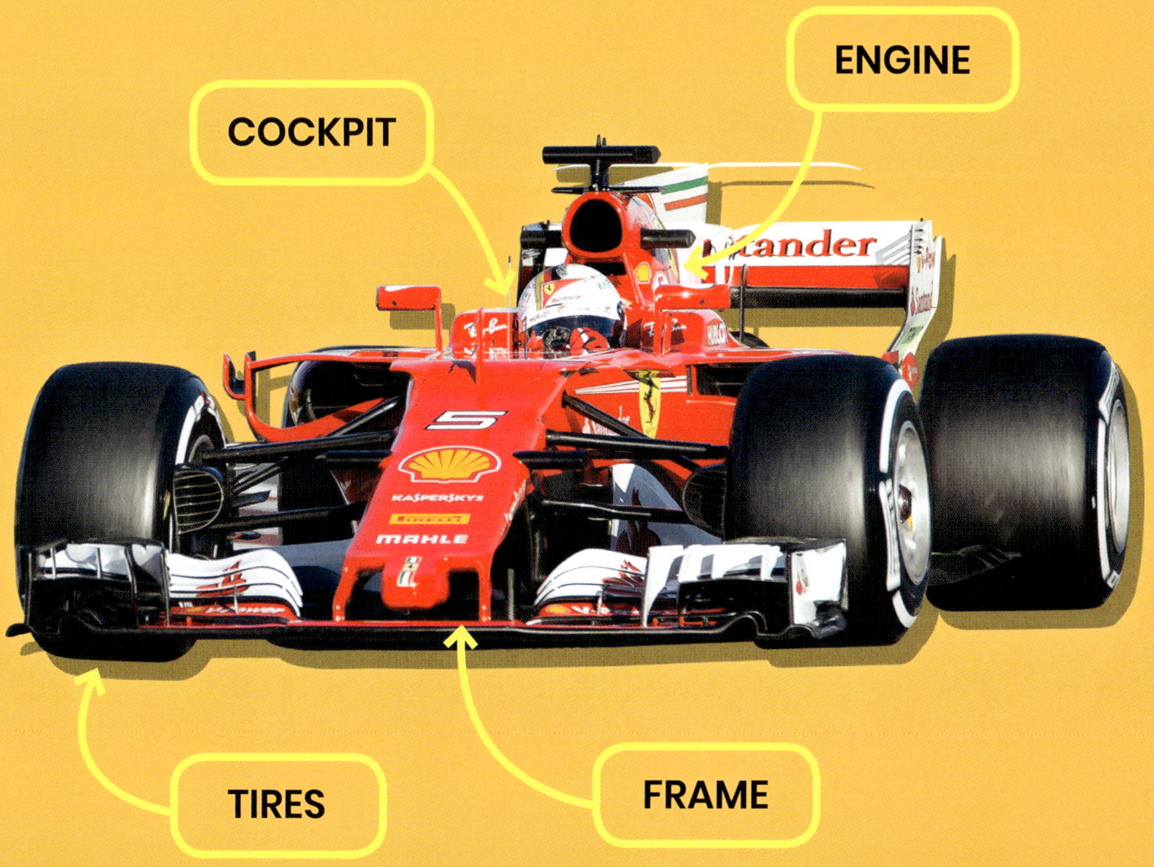

Future Cars

In the future, we will use cars that work in different ways. These cars are being fine-tuned now. Computers will help them do more things, like steer.

Solar Power

Soon, cars may run on solar power. Solar power is energy from the Sun's rays. The energy is stored in panels on the car. The car would run using only sunlight.

Driverless Cars

Some cars can drive themselves. They keep away from other cars using sensors.

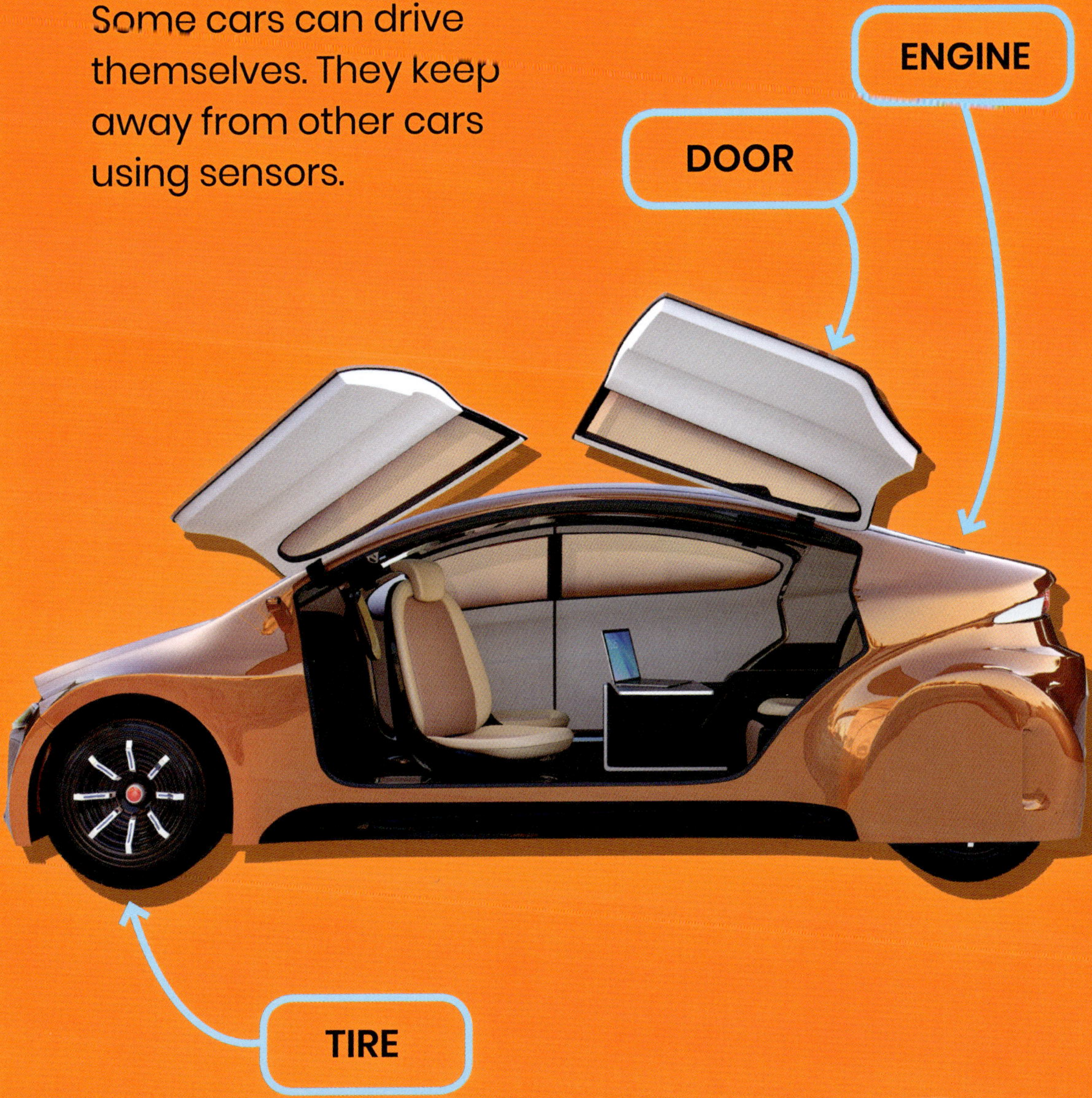

Timeline

ca. 3500 BCE	The wheel is invented.
1435	Carts and chariots are made in ancient Egypt.
43 CE	The Romans build roads in Britain.
1640s	Stagecoaches carry passengers in Britain.
1712	Thomas Newcomen invents the first steam engine.
1778	James Watts improves the steam engine. It is used widely.
1885	German Karl Benz makes the first car.
1893	The Benz Viktoria car is built.
1903	Henry Ford sets up his car factory.
1909	The Model T Ford car is developed.
1920	Half of all cars are Model T Fords.
1936	The Jaguar SS100 sports car is sold.
1950	The first Formula 1 race is held.
1960s	Big Cadillacs cruise the US highways.
1983	The first solar race cars are tested.
2010s	The first electric family cars go on sale.

Glossary

air bag A bag that fills with air if a car crashes.

combustion engine An engine that burns fuel.

computer An electric machine that works with information.

dashboard The part of a car that has controls on it. It is below the windshield.

driverless car A car that runs without a driver.

electric car A car that runs on a charged battery.

factory A big building where things are made.

fuel Something that is burned to make heat or power.

GPS A radio system that gives directions in the car.

inflate To fill something with air.

pollution When the air, water, or land gets dirty and unsafe.

seat belt A belt that holds you in place if a car stops suddenly.

sensor Something that picks up signals.

solar power Power made from the Sun's rays.

steam engine An engine that uses steam to make power. The steam is made from boiling water.

tread The thick part of a car tire. It grips the road.

Further Resources

Books

It's All about ... Fast Cars Kingfisher editors, Kingfisher, 2016

The Big Book of Things That Go DK editors, Dorling Kindersley, 2016

Who Was Henry Ford? Michael Burgan, Penguin Workshop, 2014

Websites

Learn all about the history of the car and how it works: kids.kiddle.co/Car

Check out cool facts about driverless cars: www.mocomi.com/driverless-cars/

Index